ME TOO!®
B O O K S

NOBODY KNEW BUT GOD!

MIRIAM AND BABY MOSES

By Marilyn Lashbrook

Illustrated by Stephanie McFetridge Britt

CANDLE
BOOKS

ME TOO! Books are designed to help you share the joy of reading with children. They provide a new and fun way to improve a child's reading skills – by practice and example. At the same time, you are teaching your children valuable Bible truths.

Little children can play a big part in God's plan. NOBODY KNEW BUT GOD! will help children realize the importance of fulfilling their responsibilities. They will also be reminded that when they are going through tough times, God has not forgotten them. He is working out His plan day by day. This story will present you with an opportunity to discuss with your child ways she or he can help your family...through words, actions and prayers.

Copyright © 1998 by Rainbow Studies, Inc.
All rights reserved. Printed in Italy.

ISBN 1 85985 281 5

Published in the UK by Candle Books 2000

Distributed by STL, PO Box 300, Carlisle,
Cumbria CA3 0QS

World-wide co-edition arranged by
Angus Hudson Ltd., Concorde House,
Grenville Place,
Mill Hill, London NW7 3SA
Tel: +44 20 8959 3668
Fax: +44 20 8959 3678
e-mail: coed@angushudson.com

NOBODY KNEW BUT GOD!

MIRIAM AND BABY MOSES

Taken from Exodus 1–2 and Hebrews 11:23

God's people, the Hebrews, were living in Egypt.
But the Egyptians didn't like them.

The Pharaoh of Egypt said: "There are **TOO MANY** Hebrews! Let them work for us as slaves."
And so they did.

But the Hebrews *still* grew in number. So the wicked Pharaoh said: "Every Hebrew baby boy that is born must be thrown into the Nile River!"

Now... there lived in Egypt a Hebrew girl called Miriam.
Her mother was expecting a baby.

At last the baby arrived. It was a boy!
Miriam's mum and dad didn't want to lose
their baby. So they hid him.
But it wasn't easy. . . because babies are
NOISY!

When the Egyptians weren't around,
Miriam's family took the baby out.
Miriam held her dear little brother.

Miriam's mother had a plan to keep her
baby safe.
She made a basket and coated it with tar to
keep water out.

Then she put her baby son in the basket and took him to the river. She left...and Miriam kept watch. She stayed *v-e-r-y q-u-i-e-t.*

Not long after, the princess of Egypt came to the river. She was going to bathe. Miriam was frightened for her baby brother.

"What's in that basket?" the princess
asked?
A servant brought the basket to her.
Inside was the little baby.

"It's a Hebrew boy," said the princess.
She loved the baby.

Miriam was suddenly **BRAVE**.
She went to the princess of Egypt.

"Would you like a Hebrew nurse to care for the baby?" she asked.

"Yes, please," said the princess.

So Miriam ran home to find her mum.

The princess called the baby **MOSES**.
He became her adopted son.

But she didn't know that God had a special plan for him.
NOBODY KNEW BUT GOD!
God kept baby Moses *safe...*
because one day he would lead his people out of Egypt.

So Moses was brought up by the princess of Egypt in her palace.

Read more of Moses' story in the ME TOO! BOOK title *Who Needs a Boat?*

ME TOO!®
B O O K S